HIDI
FIGURES

The True Story of Four Black Women
and the Space Race

by MARGOT LEE SHETTERLY
with WINIFRED CONKLING

illustrated by LAURA FREEMAN

SCHOLASTIC INC.

NASA

Dorothy Vaughan, Mary Jackson, Katherine Johnson, and Christine Darden were good at math. *Really* good.

In 1943, the United States was at war: World War II. Dorothy Vaughan wanted to serve her country by working for the National Advisory Committee for Aeronautics, the government agency that designed airplanes. Having the best airplanes would help America win the war. Making airplanes fly faster and higher and safer meant doing lots of tests at the agency's Langley Laboratory in Hampton, Virginia. Tests meant numbers, numbers meant math, and math meant computers.

Today we think of computers as machines, but in the 1940s, computers were actual people like Dorothy, Mary, Katherine, and Christine. Their job was to do math.

Because Dorothy was black and a woman, some people thought it would be impossible for her to get a job as a computer. She lived in Virginia, a southern state, where laws segregated, or kept apart, black people and white people.

They could not eat in the same restaurants.

They could not drink from the same water fountains.

They could not use the same restrooms.

They could not attend the same schools.

They could not play on the same sports teams.

They could not sit near each other in movie theaters.

They could not marry someone of a different race.

But Dorothy didn't think it was impossible. She was good at math. *Really* good.

She knew she was the right person for the job. She applied, and the laboratory offered her a position as a computer.

At work, blacks and whites were kept apart. The white computers worked in one building and Dorothy and the other black computers worked in a different building, in their separate office.

Even though they worked on the same kinds of assignments, the black computers and white computers used separate bathrooms and ate in separate lunchrooms.

America won the war in 1945, but Dorothy stayed on the job, still trying to make airplanes faster and safer. By 1951, the Americans and the Russians were competing to see who could build the best planes. That meant more experiments and more numbers.

Lots and lots of numbers.

And more numbers meant the need for more computers.

That's when Mary Jackson got a job as a computer at Langley. She worked in a group that tested model airplanes in wind tunnels. A wind tunnel was a machine like a huge metal box with a powerful fan attached. Mary put model airplanes in the wind tunnel and blasted them with air from the fan. This experiment helped her group improve their designs on the models before building full-sized airplanes.

Mary wanted to become an engineer, but officials said it was impossible. Most of the engineers at the laboratory were men. And to become an engineer, Mary needed to take high-level math classes, but she wasn't allowed to go inside the white school where the classes were taught.

But Mary was good at math. *Really* good. And she refused to give up. She got permission to enter the school building and take the math classes, and she earned good grades. Because she didn't give up, Mary Jackson became the first African-American female engineer at the laboratory.

HAMPTON HIGH SCHOOL

Katherine Johnson was good at math and always asked lots of questions. In 1953, she applied to the laboratory for a computer job and was placed on a team that tested actual planes while they were flying in the air. Their research was used to figure out ways to prevent future plane crashes. In one of her first projects, she learned how to analyze turbulence, or dangerous gusts of air. No one knows how many lives her work may have helped save!

Katherine wanted to help the group prepare its research reports, so she asked if she could go to meetings with the other experts on her team. Her boss told her it was impossible.

"Women aren't allowed to attend meetings," he said. But Katherine knew she was as good at math as anyone else—maybe better.

So she asked him again.

And again.

And again.

Katherine asked her boss so many times that he finally invited her to the meetings.

Katherine was good at math. *Really* good. And because she fought to be treated the same as the men, she became the first woman in her group to sign her name to one of the group's reports.

In the 1950s, the Langley laboratory bought a machine computer that could do math faster than the human computers.

At first, these machines made mistakes. Dorothy learned how to program the machines so that they got the right answers. She taught the women in her group how to program the computers, too.

In 1957, Russia launched a satellite known as *Sputnik* into orbit around the Earth. The United States started building satellites to explore space, too. For years, the laboratory had used math to design airplanes. Now it would need math to create spaceships as well. The government decided to change the agency's name from the National Advisory Committee for Aeronautics to the National Aeronautics and Space Administration—NASA!

In 1961, President John F. Kennedy told Congress, "I believe that this nation should commit itself to achieving the goal, before this decade is out, of landing a man on the moon and returning him safely to Earth."

A man on the moon! But the first step to getting a man on the moon was to send an astronaut around the Earth. NASA was going to need to hire more space experts and more people who were good at math. *Really* good.

The people at the laboratory had to work together from morning to night to figure out how to send astronaut John Glenn into space—and bring him back home to Earth safely. Katherine Johnson knew she could use math to help.

"Tell me where you want his spaceship to land, and I'll tell you where to launch it," Katherine told her boss.

Katherine helped calculate the trajectories—or pathways—that rockets traveled through space. She had to plan Glenn's *exact* route, from takeoff in Florida to splashdown in the Atlantic Ocean. There was no room for error!

No one was better than Katherine at solving these tricky math problems. Days before his mission, John Glenn wanted Katherine to double-check the machine computer's trajectory calculations, to make sure it hadn't made any mistakes.

When Katherine said the numbers were correct, Glenn was ready to go. On February 20, 1962, Glenn blasted off into space, circled the Earth, and made his way home safely.

Meanwhile, laws began to change so that black and white students could go to school together. Blacks fought for the right to sit beside whites on buses and to drink from the same water fountains. At the laboratory, black and white computers started working together in the same offices, eating at the same lunch tables, and using the same bathrooms.

Black and white moviegoers could sit next to each other in the same theater. Across the country, people started to think about ways to bring equality to *all* Americans.

Christine Darden was good at math, and she loved electronic computers. She started working at Langley in 1967. Christine wanted to become an engineer, and thanks to Dorothy, Mary, and Katherine, she knew it was possible. Eventually she became an engineer for supersonic airplanes—planes flying faster than the speed of sound. But her first job was to help with NASA's mission to the moon.

The people at the laboratory prepared for years to send astronauts to the moon—about 238,900 miles away from the Earth! Finally, on July 20, 1969, the world watched as the three men arrived at the moon in their *Apollo 11* spacecraft. "That's one small step for man, one giant leap for mankind," said astronaut Neil Armstrong when he stepped onto the dusty surface. But it was also a giant leap for Dorothy, Mary, Katherine, Christine, and all of the other computers and engineers who had worked at the laboratory over the years.

The moon landing was a success from takeoff to splashdown! But there was no time to rest. Once NASA landed astronauts on the moon, the people at the laboratory began dreaming of sending humans to other planets, such as Mars or Jupiter or Saturn. They started to imagine hyper-fast space planes that could travel around the Earth at seven times the speed of sound.

The next adventure wouldn't be easy and would require lots of tests and lots more numbers. But Dorothy, Mary, Katherine, and Christine knew one thing: with hard work, perseverance, and a love of math, *anything* was possible.

Timeline

1903
Wright Brothers
make the first powered flight

1915
Federal government establishes the National Advisory Committee for Aeronautics (NACA)

1935
First female computers are hired at Langley Memorial Aeronautical Laboratory

1939—1945 World War II

1943
Dorothy Vaughan
starts working at NACA, where she stays until 1971

1943
First African-American female computers are hired at Langley Memorial Aeronautical Laboratory

1951
Mary Jackson
starts working at NACA, where she stays until 1985

1958
National Aeronautics and Space Administration (NASA) replaces NACA

1967
Christine Darden
starts working at NASA, where she stays until 2007

1953
Katherine Johnson
starts working at NACA, where she stays until 1986

1961
Soviet cosmonaut ***Yuri Gagarin*** orbits Earth

1962
John Glenn
orbits Earth

1957
Soviet Union launches the ***Sputnik*** satellite

1969
Neil Armstrong and Edwin "Buzz" Aldrin
become first humans to land on the moon

1954
Supreme Court ***Brown v. Board of Education*** decision rules that it is unconstitutional to have separate schools for black and white students

Meet the Computers

Dorothy Johnson Vaughan (1910–2008)

Dorothy was born September 20, 1910, in Kansas City, Missouri. She and her family moved to West Virginia when she was eight. Dorothy received a full scholarship to Wilberforce University, a historically black college in Ohio, where she graduated at age nineteen with a degree in mathematics education. She married Howard Vaughan in 1932, and they had six children.

After college, Dorothy worked as a high school math teacher in Farmville, Virginia. In 1943, she began her job at Langley Memorial Aeronautical Laboratory in Hampton, Virginia. She worked as a mathematician and computer, later becoming NASA's first African-American supervisor. When machine computers were introduced at Langley, Dorothy learned the programming language FORTRAN and taught it to her staff. She died in 2008 at age ninety-eight.

Mary Winston Jackson (1921–2005)

Mary was born April 9, 1921, in Hampton, Virginia. She graduated with highest honors from the all-black Phenix High School, then graduated from Hampton Institute in 1942 with degrees in mathematics and physical science. She taught math at an all-black high school in Maryland for a year before taking a job as a bookkeeper back in her hometown. She married Levi Jackson Sr., and they had two children.

Mary began work as a computer at Langley Memorial Aeronautical Laboratory in 1951. She worked in a supersonic wind tunnel, studying the impact of wind forces that were nearly twice the speed of sound. In order to be promoted to engineer, she needed to take graduate-level courses in physics and math. She had to petition the City of Hampton, Virginia, for permission to attend the classes because they were held at a whites-only high school. She completed the classes, and in 1958 she became the first female African-American aerospace engineer at NASA. Late in her career, Mary took a position in NASA's Equal Opportunity Office, where she worked to support the careers of other women and minorities. She volunteered for more than thirty years as a Girl Scout leader. She died in 2005 at age eighty-three.

Katherine Coleman Goble Johnson (1918–2020)

Katherine was born August 26, 1918, in White Sulphur Springs, West Virginia. Her community did not offer public school for African Americans after eighth grade, so her family arranged for her to attend the high school run by West Virginia State Institute, 125 miles away. She completed high school at age fourteen and went to West Virginia State College, graduating *summa cum laude* at age eighteen with degrees in mathematics and French. In 1939, she married her first husband, Jimmy Goble, and they had three children. Jimmy Goble died of a brain tumor in 1956. Katherine married James Johnson in 1959.

Katherine taught high school math before beginning work as a computer at Langley Memorial Aeronautical Laboratory in Hampton, Virginia, in 1953. Her expertise in analytic geometry earned her a place in the Flight Research Division. She worked on the flight trajectories—the flight paths—for Project Mercury, the program that sent the first American astronauts into space. Astronaut John Glenn specifically requested that Katherine double-check the computer's calculations of his spacecraft's orbit around the Earth. She also contributed calculations to the 1969 *Apollo 11* mission to the moon. She died in 2020 at age one hundred one.

Dr. Christine Mann Darden (1942–)

Christine was born September 10, 1942, in Monroe, North Carolina. She had an early interest in understanding how things worked, and as a child she repeatedly took apart and rebuilt her bicycle. She graduated as high school valedictorian in 1958. She went to Hampton Institute on a scholarship and graduated in 1962 with a degree in mathematics education. In 1963, she married Walter Darden, Jr. She had two children and briefly taught high school math. She earned a master's degree in aerosol physics from Virginia State University. She earned her doctorate in mechanical engineering from George Washington University in 1973.

In 1967, Christine Darden began work at Langley. She became an expert on sonic booms, the sound associated with shock waves created when an object travels through the air faster than the speed of sound. She designed a computer program that could simulate sonic booms and helped improve designs of aircraft flying at supersonic speeds.

Glossary

Aeronautics: The science of flying.

Engineer: a person who has scientific training and who designs and builds machines, like airplanes.

NACA: The National Advisory Committee for Aeronautics, formed in 1915.

NASA: The National Aeronautics and Space Administration (NASA), formed in 1958.

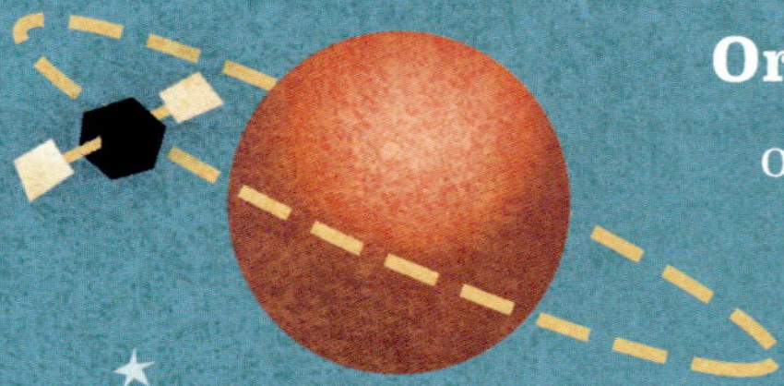

Orbit: The curved path of an object or spacecraft as it revolves around a star, planet, or moon.

Satellite: A man-made object placed in orbit around the Earth, its moon, or another planet to collect information or help with communication.

Sonic boom: The sound associated with shock waves created when an object travels through the air faster than the speed of sound.

Speed of sound: The distance traveled by a sound wave in a fixed period of time. Sound travels most slowly in gasses, faster in water, and fastest in solids.

Turbulence: A sudden jolt or shift in airflow affecting an aircraft.

Wind tunnel: A tool used in aeronautics research to study the effect of air moving over an object.

Author's Note

When I first started working on the original *Hidden Figures* book, I had no idea it would become a *New York Times* bestseller or be embraced with enthusiasm all over America by people of different ages, genders, races, ethnicities, classes, professional backgrounds, and political persuasions. But then again, when the first black women took their places in the West Area Computing Office at the Langley Memorial Aeronautical Laboratory in 1943, they had no way of knowing that those first steps would eventually help our country get to the moon.

Hidden Figures is very much a work of imagination—the kind of imagination that it took to believe that it was possible to orbit a person around the earth. The same kind of imagination that led Dr. Martin Luther King Jr. to dream of an America that would bestow the blessings of democracy on all its citizens, regardless of what they look like, where they came from, or who others perceive them to be. It's my hope that the heroines of *Hidden Figures* will spark the imaginations of the next generation of readers—and the next generation of scientists, mathematicians, and engineers—and encourage them to ride their dreams as high as their talent and determination will take them.

To my parents, Margaret G. Lee and Robert B. Lee III,
and to all the women at the NACA and NASA
who offered their shoulders to stand on

ISBN: 978-1-338-56228-6

15 16 17 18 19 40 30 29 28 27 26 25 24 23

Printed in the U.S.A.

First Scholastic printing, January 2019

Typography by Erin Fitzsimmons

Scholastic Inc., 557 Broadway, New York, NY 10012